Easy Mexican

SAVEUR

At a market in Fresnillo, Mexico, a vendor prepares gorditas, griddled masa cakes stuffed with cheese.

Easy Mexican

37 Classic Recipes

SAVEUR

BY THE EDITORS OF SAVEUR MAGAZINE

weldon**owen**

In a Mexico City grocery, Yucatecan hot sauces share shelf space with onions, sour oranges, and other foods.

TABLE OF CONTENTS

INTRODUCTION

Tacos, enchiladas, guacamole and chips: We crave these foods. How could we not? The sheer exuberance of Mexican cooking—its robust flavors, colors, and textures—seduces us. We're surprised and delighted by the lime's brightness, the chiles' sweet fire, the earthy savor of the beans. We are comforted by the soulful depth of the stews and soups, the roasted meats and rich sauces. And yet, though we love Mexican food, we hardly know it. The dishes familiar to most of us living north of the border represent a fraction of Mexico's vast repertoire of regional flavors. From the fresh seafood of Veracruz to the bold spice pastes of the Yucatán to the Sonoran desert's smoky grilled beef, you can taste the diversity—and the history—in the country's dishes. These are foods with a deep lineage. A simple corn tortilla holds within it the heritage of the Aztecs. But as intense and complex as Mexican flavors are, one of the cuisine's greatest surprises is how easy it is to cook. With some basic techniques, detailed in this book, you can make these recipes your own. What a joy it is to celebrate Mexico in our very own kitchens. —*THE EDITORS*

Arculano Valenzuela, of San Pablo, Mexico, enjoys a bowl of Mexican red rice (see page 81 for a recipe).

In Juchitan, a vendor prepares *bu'pu,* a drink that is usually eaten with a spoon and can only be found in that part of Mexico, consisting of *atole blanco* (corn porridge) covered in foam made from cacao and plumeria flowers.

A GUIDE TO MEXICAN DRIED CHILES

Spicy native chiles, preserved through sun-drying, heat-drying, or smoking, are a cornerstone of Mexican cooking. Drying concentrates sweetness, deepens pungency, and adds complex layers of flavor, which the chiles impart to countless dishes. ❶ Sweet, sharp anchos—dried poblano peppers—are soaked (see "How to Soak Chiles," page 42) and stuffed or toasted and ground for sauces and soups. ❷ Raisin-flavored pasillas are used in moles or soaked and paired with cream sauces. ❸ Puyas add a kick when ground into sauces and stews. ❹ Cascabel's earthy spice enhances table sauces. ❺ Chile meco, a smoky chipotle, lends savoriness to sauces. ❻ Mellow mulato negros bring chocolaty depth to moles. ❼ Chipotles lend woodsy heat to marinades and sauces. ❽ Guajillos offer piquancy to table sauces, stews, and rubs. ❾ Fiery chiles de árbol are added whole to soups and stews, or are ground to spice up salsas and marinades.

Starters

In Mexico, there's an easy starter for every appetite, from addictive dips and fresh seafood to soul-satisfying soups and earthy snacks.

GUACAMOLE

MAKES ABOUT 4 CUPS

This simple recipe showcases the pure flavor of ripe avocados. Though guacamole is traditionally prepared in a *molcajete*, a Mexican version of a mortar and pestle, a fork and metal bowl work just as well for mashing the soft fruit.

¼   cup finely chopped white onion

2   tbsp. minced cilantro

4   serrano chiles, stemmed, seeded, and finely chopped

2   cloves garlic, minced

    Kosher salt, to taste

3   ripe avocados, halved, pitted, peeled, and cut into 1" chunks

1   plum tomato, cored, seeded, and finely chopped

    Juice of 1 lime

    Tortilla chips, for serving

1 In a large bowl, combine onion, cilantro, chiles, and garlic; sprinkle heavily with salt and mash with a fork into a slightly chunky paste.

2 Add avocados, tomato, and juice, and stir to combine, mashing some of the avocado slightly as you stir. Season with salt, and serve at once with tortilla chips.

Cooking Note *Guacamole is best served right away, but to keep leftovers bright green, press a piece of plastic wrap directly onto the surface; this keeps air out that will oxidize and turn the guacamole brown. Store it in the refrigerator until you're ready to serve it again.*

TORTILLA SOUP

Sopa de Tortilla

SERVES 6

This substantive soup is a beloved dish in Mexico City and other parts of Central Mexico. Sliced scallions, mashed avocados, minced chiles and cilantro, and myriad other toppings can be used to garnish it just before serving.

8 cloves garlic, smashed

1 large white onion, cut into 1" wedges

2 chipotle chiles in adobo sauce, store-bought or homemade

1 28-oz. can whole, peeled tomatoes with juice

5 cups chicken stock

6 tbsp. fresh lime juice

Kosher salt and freshly ground black pepper, to taste

Corn tortilla chips, store-bought or homemade

½ cup crema or sour cream

1½ cups crumbled queso fresco or feta cheese

1 Heat a 6-qt. Dutch oven over high heat. Add garlic and onion wedges, and cook, turning once, until charred on both sides, about 8 minutes. Remove from the heat and transfer to a blender along with chipotles and tomatoes; purée until smooth.

2 Return sauce to pot and bring to a boil over medium-high heat; cook, stirring, until slightly reduced, about 8 minutes. Add stock, reduce heat to medium-low, and cook, stirring occasionally, to meld flavors, about 10 minutes. Add juice, and season with salt and pepper.

3 Place a handful of chips in each serving bowl and pour soup over top. Drizzle with crema and sprinkle with cheese; serve immediately.

Cooking Note *Store-bought tortilla chips make a convenient alternative to homemade ones. We like Xochitl White Corn Chips, which have a fresh corn taste and light but sturdy heft.*

SQUASH BLOSSOM QUESADILLAS

Quesadillas de Flor de Calabaza

SERVES 4

Delicate squash blossoms are a delicious filling for quesadillas, traditionally made with *queso Oaxaca,* a stringy cows' milk cheese that resembles mozzarella.

2	cups grated Oaxaca or mozzarella cheese
4	6" corn tortillas
8	fresh squash blossoms
	Kosher salt and freshly ground black pepper, to taste
2	tbsp. canola oil
	Mashed avocado, for serving
	Crumbled queso fresco or feta cheese, to garnish
	Salsa, for serving (optional)

1 Place ½ cup grated cheese over one half of each tortilla. Trim squash blossoms at the base to remove their stems, and remove and discard the tube-like stamens inside each flower. Arrange 2 squash blossoms over the cheese on each tortilla, overlapping them slightly. Season with salt and pepper, and fold each tortilla over blossoms and cheese to form a half moon.

2 Heat 1 tbsp. canola oil in a 12" skillet over medium-high heat. Add 2 quesadillas, and cook, flipping once, until cheese is melted and quesadilla is golden brown on both sides, about 5 minutes. Repeat with remaining oil and quesadillas. Transfer to a plate, top with avocado and queso fresco. Serve immediately, along with your favorite salsa, if you like.

Cooking Note *These all purpose quesadillas work well with any filling. If squash blossoms are not available, try cooked and crumbled chorizo, caramelized onions and mushrooms, or sautéed kale.*

FAVA BEAN SOUP

Sopa de Habas

SERVES 4

The secret to this soup is an aromatic base of tomatoes, garlic, and onions—called a *recaudo*—that is puréed and sautéed before the beans are added to the pot.

2   cups shelled, dried fava beans

1   plum tomato, cored and roughly chopped

1   clove garlic, roughly chopped

1   small white onion, roughly chopped

Kosher salt and freshly ground black pepper, to taste

1   tbsp. olive oil

¼   tsp. crushed saffron threads (optional)

¼   tsp. ground cumin

Roughly chopped cilantro, to garnish

Tomato and Chile Salsa (see page 31 for a recipe), to garnish

1 Bring fava beans and 4 cups water to a boil in a 4-qt. saucepan over high heat. Reduce heat to medium-low, and cook, covered and stirring, until tender, about 40 minutes.

2 Meanwhile, make the recaudo: Combine tomato, garlic, half the onion, and salt and pepper in a blender or food processor and purée until smooth; set aside.

3 Heat oil in another 4-qt. saucepan over medium-high heat. Add recuado, and cook, stirring constantly, until it begins to thicken, about 5 minutes.

4 Add the fava beans along with their cooking liquid, saffron, if using, and cumin. Bring to a boil, reduce heat to medium, and cook, stirring occasionally, until flavors meld and beans are very tender and break up in the soup, about 10 minutes. Divide soup among serving bowls and sprinkle with remaining onions and cilantro. Drizzle with salsa, if you like, before serving.

Cooking Note *Make sure to purchase dried fava beans for which the skin has been removed; the package label should clearly indicate whether or not it has been. Fava beans in their skins take twice as long to cook and need to be peeled once they're done.*

GRILLED BEAN AND CHEESE SANDWICHES

Molletes

SERVES 8

The *bolillo,* a white bread loaf from Mexico, is the foundation of this comforting snack, a great way to use leftover beans; a kaiser roll works just as well.

FOR THE SALSA:

- 2 lb. plum tomatoes, cored, and cut into ½" cubes
- ⅔ cup roughly chopped cilantro leaves
- 6 serrano or 4 jalapeño chiles, stemmed, seeded, and finely chopped
- 1 large white onion, finely chopped

  Kosher salt and freshly ground black pepper, to taste

FOR THE BEANS AND ROLLS:

- ½ cup canola oil
- 4 cloves garlic, minced
- 1 small white onion, finely chopped
- 2 cups chicken stock
- 3 15-oz. cans pinto beans, drained and rinsed

  Kosher salt and freshly ground black pepper, to taste
- 4 Kaiser rolls
- 12 oz. Chihuahua or Monterey Jack cheese, grated

1 To make the salsa, combine tomatoes, cilantro, chiles, and onion in a bowl and season liberally with salt and pepper; fold gently to combine. Cover and refrigerate to blend flavors, about 1 hour.

2 To make the refried beans, heat oil in a 12" skillet over medium-high heat. Add garlic and onion, and cook, stirring, until soft, about 8 minutes. Add stock and beans, and cook, stirring and mashing, until almost all beans are smooth and mixture is slightly soupy, about 5 minutes. Season with salt and pepper, and keep warm.

3 Heat broiler to high. Split each roll horizontally, and scoop out the insides from the tops and bottoms, leaving about a ½"-thick shell; discard insides. Place roll halves on a foil-lined baking sheet with their cut sides up, and broil until lightly toasted, about 2 minutes. Pour about ½ cup refried beans over each roll half so that the beans are spilling over the edges, and then sprinkle with cheese. Return to broiler and heat until beans are heated through and cheese is just melted, but not browned, about 2 minutes.

4 Transfer one roll half to each serving plate and top each with a couple large spoonfuls of salsa. Serve immediately.

Cooking Note *In a pinch, canned refried beans and store-bought pico de gallo can be used to make this quick and satisfying dish, which is sometimes served at breakfast.*

MEXICAN CORN ON THE COB

Elotes

SERVES 4

Adding cilantro to the boiling water lends an herbal flavor to this mayonnaise-slathered, chile-spiked corn, a popular Mexican street snack.

	Kosher salt, to taste
4	ears corn, in husks
8	sprigs cilantro
4	tbsp. unsalted butter, softened
½	cup mayonnaise
1⅓	cups crumbled Cotija or feta cheese
4	tsp. ancho chile powder
1	lime, cut into 4 wedges

1 Bring a 6-qt. saucepan of salted water to a boil over high heat. Add corn and cilantro, and cook until corn is tender, about 30 minutes. Remove corn from water and let cool briefly.

2 If you'd like to grill the corn after boiling it, build a medium-hot fire in a charcoal grill or heat a gas grill to medium-high. (Alternatively, heat a cast-iron grill pan over medium-high heat.) Peel back the husks on each boiled ear of corn, and place on grill; cook, turning as needed, until lightly charred, about 2 minutes.

3 Using a pastry brush, spread 1 tbsp. butter evenly over each ear. Brush with 2 tbsp. mayonnaise and sprinkle with ⅓ cup cheese and 1 tsp. chile powder. Serve with lime wedges.

Cooking Note *If you prefer, once the corn is grilled, cut the kernels off the cob into a large bowl and toss them with the remaining ingredients. Spoon the mixture into small cups for a warm corn salad.*

SHRIMP CEVICHE

Ceviche de Camarones

SERVES 4–6

At beachside eateries in Veracruz and in the *cevicherias* of
Mexico City, this lime-cured seafood dish is a popular snack.

1½ lb. small, raw shrimp,
peeled, deveined, tails
removed, and roughly
chopped

½ cup thinly sliced
cilantro leaves

1 tsp. worcestershire

1 jalapeño, stemmed,
seeded, and finely
chopped

½ small red onion, minced

Juice of 3 limes

Kosher salt, to taste

1 ripe avocado, pitted,
peeled, and cut into
½" cubes

Saltine crackers,
for serving

1 In a large bowl, combine shrimp, cilantro, worcestershire, jalapeño, onion, and juice; cover and refrigerate for at least 2 hours and up to 4 hours, tossing every half hour to ensure the shrimp are evenly covered in juice.

2 When ready to serve, transfer to a serving bowl, and season with salt. Top with avocado and serve with crackers.

Cooking Note *Try not to prepare the ceviche too far in advance. The shrimp will get rubbery if they sit in the marinade longer than 4 hours.*

Salsas

A ubiquitous element of Mexican cuisine, these quick, bright condiments enhance the flavor of everything from crisp tortilla chips to roasted meats and stews.

TOMATO AND CHILE SALSA

Salsa Roja

MAKES ABOUT 2 CUPS

Toasting the vegetables in this salsa on a dry, hot skillet brings out their sweetness and gives them a silky texture; it also mellows the chiles' heat and lends them a complex depth.

10	dried guajillo chiles
6	dried chiles de árbol
3	cloves garlic, peeled
2	plum tomatoes, cored
1	small white onion, halved
	Kosher salt, to taste

1 Heat a 12" skillet over high heat. Add dried guajillo chiles and chiles de árbol (see "A Guide to Mexican Dried Chiles," page 10), and cook, turning as needed, until lightly toasted all over, about 1 minute. Transfer to a bowl and cover with boiling water; let sit until chiles soften, about 20 minutes. Drain chiles, reserving 1 cup soaking liquid, and remove stems and seeds. Transfer chiles and reserved soaking liquid to a blender and set aside.

2 Return skillet to high heat. Add garlic, tomatoes, and onion, and cook, turning as needed, until blackened all over, about 6 minutes for garlic, 15 minutes for tomatoes, and 12 minutes for onion.

3 Transfer to blender with chiles along with salt, and purée until smooth and silky, at least 2 minutes. Transfer to a bowl and let cool to room temperature before serving.

Cooking Note *To turn this into a quick roasted tomato and chile soup, simply combine the salsa and 6 cups chicken stock in a 4-qt. saucepan, and cook over medium-high heat for about 10 minutes.*

TOMATILLO SALSA

Salsa Verde

MAKES ABOUT 4 CUPS

This bright, fruity salsa is the perfect counterpoint to the richness
of cheesy quesadillas and grilled meats and fish.

4	oz. tomatillos, husked and rinsed
4	cloves garlic
2	medium white onions, quartered
2	jalapeños, stemmed
1	tsp. sugar
1	bunch cilantro, stemmed
	Kosher salt and freshly ground black pepper, to taste

1 Place tomatillos, garlic, onions, and jalapeños in a 4-qt. saucepan and cover with water by 1". Bring to a boil over high heat, and cook until slightly soft, about 5 minutes. Drain vegetables, and reserve 1 cup cooking liquid.

2 Transfer to a blender along with reserved liquid, sugar, cilantro, and salt and pepper, and purée until smooth. Transfer to a serving bowl and let cool to room temperature before serving.

Cooking Note *Boiling the vegetables for this salsa helps remove some of their sharp flavors, which can be overpowering; it also helps to set the jalapeños' bright green color.*

HOMEMADE CHIPOTLES
IN ADOBO SAUCE
MAKES ABOUT 4 CUPS

Chipotle chiles (smoke dried jalapeños) marinated in tangy adobo sauce
are eaten as a condiment on tortas, quesadillas, and alongside rice and
beans, and other dishes.

4	oz. dried chipotle (mora) chiles
3	dried ancho chiles
¾	cup distilled white vinegar
⅓	cup white wine vinegar
⅓	cup rice wine vinegar
⅓	cup packed dark brown sugar
1	tbsp. kosher salt
¼	tsp. dried marjoram
¼	tsp. dried thyme
¼	tsp. lightly crushed cumin seeds
4	cloves garlic, roughly chopped
1	bay leaf
2	tbsp. canola oil

1 Pierce chipotle chiles a few times with the tip of a knife and place in a 6-qt. saucepan; cover with water and bring to a boil over high heat. Reduce heat to low, and cook, covered, until chiles are soft, about 30 minutes; drain, remove stems, and set aside. Place ancho chiles in a bowl and cover with 2 cups boiling water; let sit until rehydrated, about 20 minutes. Drain, remove stems, and transfer to a blender, along with 4 of the reserved chipotle chiles, vinegars, sugar, salt, marjoram, thyme, cumin, garlic, and bay leaf; puree sauce until smooth.

2 Heat oil in a 12" skillet over medium-high heat. Add sauce, and cook, stirring constantly, until sauce comes to a boil; add remaining chipotle chiles, reduce heat to medium, and cook until sauce thickens slightly, about 15 minutes. Transfer chiles and sauce to a sterilized 1-qt. glass jar with lid and seal; store in the refrigerator up to 3 months.

PEANUT AND CHILE SALSA

Salsa de Cacahuate y Chile de Árbol

MAKES ABOUT 1½ CUPS

A traditional salsa from Chiapas, Mexico, this smooth peanut sauce is delicious spooned on roast chicken or grilled shrimp.

¼ cup canola oil

½ cup roasted, unsalted peanuts

2 tbsp. sesame seeds

10 dried chiles de árbol, stemmed

1 dried guajillo chile, stemmed

8 cloves garlic, finely chopped

1 small white onion, finely chopped

1 tbsp. apple cider vinegar

1 tsp. dried oregano, preferably Mexican

Kosher salt, to taste

1 Heat oil in a 12" skillet over medium-high heat. Add peanuts, sesame seeds, both chiles, garlic, and onion, and cook, stirring, until onions are soft and peanuts are lightly browned, about 8 minutes. Remove from the heat and let cool to room temperature.

2 Transfer to a blender along with vinegar, oregano, salt, and 1 cup water, and purée until smooth. Transfer to a serving bowl, and let cool to room temperature before serving.

Cooking Note *Don't be tempted to use peanut butter as a substitute to make this salsa. Fresh, toasted peanuts are the key to getting the right deep, round flavor.*

PUMPKIN SEED SALSA

Sikil P'ak

MAKES ABOUT 1½ CUPS

This salsa from the Yucatán is thicker and creamier than most.
It makes a great dip for fresh vegetables.

1¼ cups raw, unhulled pumpkin seeds

2 plum tomatoes, cored

1 habanero or Scotch bonnet chile, stemmed

3 tbsp. finely chopped cilantro

3 tbsp. finely chopped chives

Kosher salt, to taste

1 Heat an 8" skillet over medium-high heat. Add pumpkin seeds, and cook, swirling pan often, until lightly toasted, about 3 minutes. Transfer to a food processor and process until smooth, about 45 seconds; set aside.

2 Return skillet to heat and add tomatoes and chile; cook, turning as needed, until charred all over, about 5 minutes for the chile, 7 minutes for the tomatoes. Transfer to food processor with pumpkin seeds along with cilantro, chives, and salt, and pulse until smooth.

3 Transfer to a bowl and cover with plastic wrap. Store in the refrigerator until ready to serve. Serve at room temperature.

Cooking Note *If you like thinner salsa, add up to 1 cup of vegetable stock or water to the mixture in the food processor.*

PICO DE GALLO WITH SHRIMP

MAKES ABOUT 6½ CUPS

In coastal Oaxaca, both fresh and dried shrimp appear in all kinds of dishes. Here, cooked shrimp bring substance and a sweet, briny disposition to a classic pico de gallo.

2   lb. plum tomatoes, cored and roughly chopped

8   oz. cooked small shrimp, peeled, and roughly chopped

½   cup roughly chopped pickled jalapeños, plus ¼ cup brine from jar

½   cup roughly chopped cilantro

1   small white onion, roughly chopped

Juice of 3 limes

Kosher salt, to taste

1 In a large bowl, combine tomatoes, shrimp, jalapeños plus brine, cilantro, onion, and juice. Season with salt and let sit at room temperature for at least 1 hour to blend flavors before serving.

Cooking Note *A sturdy salsa like this is great with chips, but even better served over grilled vegetables, white fish, or simply wrapped in tortillas as a snack.*

HOW TO SOAK CHILES

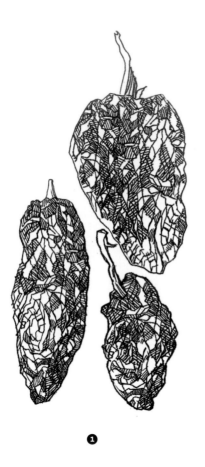

❶ **1**

❷ **2**

❶ Dried chiles have countless uses in the kitchen (see "A Guide to Mexican Dried Chiles," page 10). When toasted and ground, they become potent and versatile spices, and when soaked and softened, they make a delicious base for sauces, from the spicy, silky sauce for the pork on page 67 to the nutty, complex mole poblano on page 51. Soaking and cleaning dried chiles is quick and easy. Here's how to do it: ❷ Put the chiles into a bowl and cover them with boiling water.

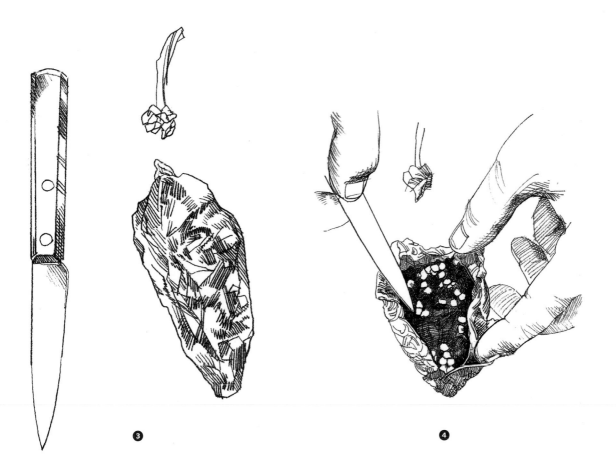

③

④

Let them soak, nudging them occasionally with a spoon to make sure they're fully submerged, until the chiles are soft, about 20 minutes. ❸ Remove them from the water, and pull off the stems. ❹ Finally, slice the chiles open lengthwise, and scrape out the seeds. (The seeds may be reserved for another use, such as adding them to a mole poblano to rachet up its heat.) The chiles are now ready to purée.

FRESH PINEAPPLE SALSA

Salsa de Piña Picante

MAKES ABOUT 1⅓ CUPS

Roberto Santibañez, chef-owner of the Fonda restaurants in New York City, gave us the recipe for this chunky, sweet-tart salsa, an ideal foil for rich meats.

1	cup finely chopped fresh pineapple
¼	cup finely chopped cilantro
3	tbsp. fresh lime juice
2	tbsp. fresh orange juice
1½	tsp. sugar
1	tsp. kosher salt
2	jalapeños, stemmed and minced
½	small red onion, minced

1 In a large bowl, mix together all the ingredients. Cover with plastic wrap and store in the refrigerator to allow flavors to meld, at least 1 hour. Serve at room temperature.

Cooking Note *Avoid using canned pineapple to make this salsa; it lacks the firmness and vivacity of the fresh fruit, whose sweet flavor balances perfectly with this salsa's other ingredients.*

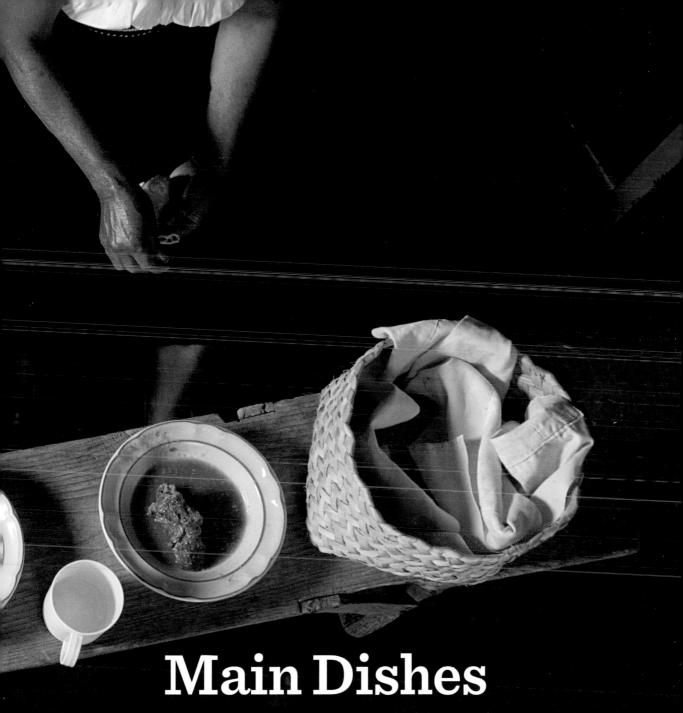

Main Dishes

Juicy meats and gooey cheeses, sauces fragrant with spices, earthy potatoes, and more make the following foods so satisfying, you won't believe how easy they are to prepare.

PORK AND BLACK BEAN STEW

Frijol con Puerco

SERVES 6–8

This recipe, from Jorge Boneta, formerly the chef at the Hotel Matilda
in San Miguel de Allende, calls for cooking the pork and beans together,
a time-saving technique that also enhances the flavor of each ingredient.

½   cup canola oil

2   lb. boneless pork shoulder,
cut into 2" cubes

Kosher salt and freshly
ground black pepper,
to taste

8   cloves garlic, finely
chopped

2   medium white onions,
thinly sliced

1   lb. dried black beans,
soaked overnight

4   sprigs cilantro

1   lb. plum tomatoes,
cored

2   habanero or Scotch
bonnet chiles, stemmed

2   baby radishes, very thinly
sliced, to garnish

Fresh purslane or
cilantro, to garnish

Cooked white rice,
for serving

Lime wedges, for serving

1 Heat 2 tbsp. oil in a 6-qt. saucepan over medium-high heat.
Season pork with salt and pepper, and working in batches,
add to pan, and cook, turning as needed, until browned on
all sides, about 6 minutes. Using a slotted spoon, transfer
pork to a plate; cover and set aside. Add ⅔ of the garlic,
¼ of the onions to pan, and cook, stirring until soft, about
5 minutes. Return pork to pot along with beans, cilantro, and
8 cups water, and bring to a boil. Reduce heat to medium,
and cook, stirring occasionally, until beans and pork are
tender, about 1 hour and 15 minutes.

2 Meanwhile, heat a 12" skillet over medium-high heat.
Add tomatoes and chiles, and cook, turning as needed, until
blackened all over, about 12 minutes. Transfer to a blender
along with remaining garlic and onions, and purée until
sauce is smooth. Return skillet to heat and add remaining oil;
when the oil is hot, add sauce, and cook, stirring constantly,
until sauce is reduced slightly, about 8 minutes. Season with
salt and pepper, and keep tomato sauce warm.

3 To serve, transfer beans and pork to a large, deep
serving platter and drizzle with tomato sauce. Top with
radishes and purslane, and serve with rice and lime
wedges on the side.

Cooking Note *Substitute one pound of any dried beans you
like for the black beans. Pintos, navy beans, and even black-
eyed peas work well in this dish.*

QUICK CHICKEN MOLE POBLANO

SERVES 8

In Puebla, where this intensely flavorful dish originated, it can take
days to prepare. Our simplified recipe yields a mole that is as delicious
and complexly flavored as one made using traditional methods.

4   oz. dried pasilla chiles

1   3 4-lb. whole chicken,
     cut into 8 pieces

2   tbsp. unsalted butter

2   cloves garlic, chopped

½   plum tomato, cored
     and chopped

½   tomatillo, husk removed,
     rinsed, and chopped

¼   small white onion,
     chopped

¼   tsp. each ground cloves,
     allspice, cinnamon,
     coriander, anise seeds,
     and black pepper

2   tbsp. whole almonds

2   tbsp. raisins

1½   tbsp. sesame seeds,
     plus more to garnish

½   corn tortilla,
     torn into pieces

½   slice stale white bread,
     toasted and crumbled

¼   ripe plantain or banana,
     peeled and finely chopped

1   tbsp. canola oil

2   oz. Mexican chocolate,
     roughly chopped

1   tbsp. light brown sugar

¾   tbsp. kosher salt

     Mexican rice, for serving
     (see page 81 for a recipe;
     optional)

1 Heat a 12" skillet over medium-high heat. Add chiles, and
cook, turning once, until toasted, about 2 minutes. Transfer
chiles to a large bowl; pour over 10 cups boiling water and
let sit until chiles soften, about 30 minutes. Drain, reserving
soaking liquid, and remove stems and seeds, reserving 2 tsp.
seeds. Purée chiles and 2 cups soaking liquid in a blender
until smooth. Set chile purée and remaining soaking liquid
aside. Bring chicken and 8 cups water to a boil in a 4-qt.
saucepan over high heat, reduce heat to medium-low, and
cook until cooked through, about 30 minutes. Drain and
keep warm.

2 Heat butter in a 4-qt. saucepan over medium-high heat.
Add garlic, tomato, tomatillo, and onion, and cook, stirring,
until soft, about 8 minutes. Add reserved chile seeds, cloves,
allspice, cinnamon, coriander, anise, and pepper, and cook,
stirring constantly, until fragrant, about 1 minute. Add
almonds, raisins, sesame seeds, tortilla, bread, and plantain,
and cook, stirring, until lightly toasted, about 7 minutes.
Add reserved chile purée, and bring to a boil; reduce heat
to medium-low and cook until all ingredients are softened,
about 20 minutes. Remove from heat, and working in
batches, transfer mole to blender along with remaining
soaking liquid, and purée until smooth, at least 4 minutes.

3 Heat oil in a 6-qt. saucepan over medium-high heat. Add
mole, and cook, whisking constantly, until slightly thickened,
about 5 minutes. Add chocolate, sugar, and salt, and cook
until smooth and flavors meld, about 10 minutes. Spoon the
mole over chicken to serve, and sprinkle with sesame seeds.
Serve with Mexican rice, if you like.

CHICKEN IN GREEN CHILE SAUCE

Pollo Horneado

SERVES 8

Stained orange from the spice achiote (also known as annatto), this flavorful grilled chicken gets served with a bright jalapeño and onion relish.

2 tbsp. prepared yellow mustard

2 tbsp. kosher salt, plus more to taste

1 tbsp. ground achiote

10 cloves garlic, peeled

5 guajillo chiles, stemmed and seeded

Juice of 1 lime

1 3–4-lb. whole chicken, cut into 8 pieces

½ cup chicken stock

6 jalapeños, stemmed, seeded, and roughly chopped

1 small white onion, finely chopped

1 Combine mustard, salt, achiote, garlic, chiles, juice, and 1 cup boiling water in a blender and purée until very smooth, at least 1 minute. Transfer to large bowl, and add chicken; toss to coat, and then cover and let marinate in the refrigerator at least 4 hours or overnight. Meanwhile, combine stock, jalapeños, and half the onion in a food processor and purée until smooth. Transfer to a bowl and stir in remaining onion. Season with salt, and set salsa aside.

2 Build a medium-hot fire in a charcoal grill or heat a gas grill to medium. (Alternatively, heat a cast-iron grill pan over medium-high heat.) Remove chicken from marinade, and working in batches, add chicken to grill, and cook, turning once, until charred in spots and cooked through, about 25 minutes. Transfer to a serving platter, and serve with salsa on the side.

Cooking Note *If you're cooking the chicken on a charcoal or gas grill, you can soak hickory, mesquite, or other hardwood chips in water overnight and add them to the coal fire to impart a smoky flavor to the dish.*

MEXICAN NOODLE CASSEROLE

Sopa Seca

SERVES 8

Angela Tovar Morales (pictured, at left), a cook at La Casa Dragones in San Miguel de Allende, Mexico, gave us the recipe for this oven-baked dish lavished with *crema* (a mild Mexican sour cream) and cheese.

¼ cup olive oil, plus more for greasing

12 oz. dried fideo noodles or angel hair pasta, broken into 3" lengths

1 medium white onion, thinly sliced

1 tsp. ground coriander

¼ tsp. cumin seeds

1 tsp. dried oregano, preferably Mexican

1 tsp. chili powder

6 cloves garlic, minced

1 bay leaf

1½ cups canned whole peeled tomatoes drained and crushed

3 chipotle chiles in adobo sauce, store bought or homemade, minced

1 sprig cilantro, plus 1 tbsp. minced, for garnish

2 cups chicken stock

Kosher salt and freshly ground black pepper, to taste

1 cup crumbled Cotija or feta cheese

1 cup crema or sour cream

Sautéed cactus or green beans for serving (optional)

1 Heat the oven to 375°. Grease an 8" x 8" baking dish with oil; set aside. Heat ¼ cup oil in a 12" skillet over medium-high heat. Working in two batches, add pasta and cook, stirring, until lightly browned and toasted, about 4 minutes. Using a slotted spoon, transfer to paper towels to drain; set aside.

2 Return skillet to heat, and add onion; cook, stirring, until soft, about 4 minutes. Add the coriander, cumin, oregano, chili powder, garlic, and bay leaf, and cook, stirring, until fragrant, about 30 seconds. Add tomatoes, chipotles, and cilantro sprig, and cook until thickened, about 5 minutes. Add reserved noodles and stock, season with salt and pepper, and bring to a boil; reduce heat to medium-low, and cook, stirring, until noodles are al dente, about 6 minutes. Remove from the heat and pour into prepared dish; sprinkle with cheese. Bake until cheese is soft, about 15 minutes.

3 Drizzle with crema and sprinkle with minced cilantro; serve with sautéed cactus or green beans, tossed with pico de gallo, if you like.

Cooking Note *Any long, thin, broken-up pasta will work here in a pinch, including vermicelli or spaghetti.*

MAKING CORN TORTILLAS

Store-bought corn tortillas make a fine canvas for the squash blossom quesadillas on page 19, the carne asada tacos on page 60, the enchiladas suizas on page 71, and scores of other dishes. But once you taste a homemade tortilla, you'll instantly notice the difference: Fragrant, toasty, and supple, fresh tortillas are unparalleled in quality. Making them couldn't be simpler. Here's how to do it:

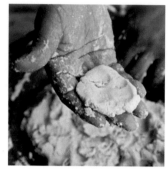

❶ Heat a cast-iron skillet or griddle over medium heat. Place 1 cup masa harina (sold under the brand name Maseca) into a bowl and make a well in center. Add ⅔ cup plus 1 tbsp. water to well, and stir with a fork to form a dough.

❷ Knead the dough until soft but not sticky; it should have the consistency of damp earth or Play-Doh. Pinch off a golf ball–size piece, and roll it into a ball.

❸ Cut two circles 7" in diameter out of a clean plastic bag. Put 1 circle on the bottom plate of a tortilla press (find these online at Amazon.com). Place dough ball in the center, and top it with the second plastic circle.

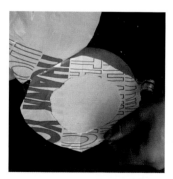

❹ Cover with the top plate of tortilla press, and press the handle down on tortilla press to flatten the dough.

❺ Open press; remove top piece of plastic. Transfer tortilla to palm of your hand; peel plastic from bottom.

6 Place the tortilla immediately in the skillet and cook until it begins to brown and blister on the bottom. Quickly flip the tortilla and continue cooking until lightly toasted on the other side (the tortilla may also puff up). Transfer the tortilla to a bowl or container lined with a kitchen towel, and cover with towel to keep warm. Repeat with the remainder of the dough. Makes about 8 tortillas.

CHICKEN AND POTATO STEW

Pollo Guisado

SERVES 6

Different versions of this comforting dish are made all over
Latin America. Mexican cooks like to include a combination of
chiles, which lends the stew a complex flavor.

¼	cup canola oil
1½	lb. boneless, skinless chicken thighs
	Kosher salt and freshly ground black pepper, to taste
1	small white onion, chopped
1	medium carrot, chopped
1	red bell pepper, stemmed, seeded, and finely chopped
1	tsp. ground cumin
1	tsp. dried thyme
6	cloves garlic, minced
2	chipotles in adobo sauce, store-bought or home-made, finely chopped
1	jalapeño, quartered lengthwise
1	lb. Yukon gold potatoes, peeled, cut into ½" cubes
4	cups chicken stock
3	sprigs cilantro
1	15-oz. can whole peeled tomatoes in juice, crushed
3	tbsp. capers, rinsed
	Juice of 1 lime

1 Heat oil in a 6-qt. saucepan over medium-high heat. Season chicken with salt and pepper, and working in batches, add to pan, and cook, turning once, until browned on both sides and cooked through, about 15 minutes. Transfer to a plate and let cool; using a fork, finely shred meat and set aside.

2 Return saucepan to heat, and add onion, carrot, and bell pepper; cook, stirring, until soft, about 8 minutes. Add cumin, thyme, garlic, chipotles, and jalapeño, and cook, stirring, until fragrant, about 2 minutes. Add reserved shredded chicken back to pan along with potatoes, stock, cilantro, and tomatoes, and bring to a boil; reduce heat to medium-low, and cook, stirring occasionally, until potatoes are tender, about 30 minutes. Add capers, juice, and season with salt and pepper before serving.

Cooking Note *To make the dish even simpler to prepare, you can use leftover roast chicken or pork shredded into bite-size pieces in place of the chicken thighs. Simply skip step 1, and add the leftover meat to the stew as you would the shredded chicken thighs.*

CARNE ASADA TACOS

SERVES 4

*Skirt steak, a full-flavored and juicy cut, is an excellent choice
for* carne asada; *marinated with lime and spices before grilling,
the beef pairs nicely with a tart* salsa verde.

3   tbsp. canola oil

6   canned chipotles in adobo
sauce, roughly chopped

4   cloves garlic, finely
chopped

1   large white onion, sliced
crosswise into ¾"-thick
rings, plus 1 small white
onion, roughly chopped

Juice of 2 limes, plus lime
wedges for serving

1½ lb. trimmed skirt steak,
cut crosswise into
4 steaks

Kosher salt and freshly
ground black pepper,
to taste

1   jalapeño, stemmed

Warm tortillas,
for serving

Tomatillo Salsa, for
serving (see page 32
for a recipe; optional)

Pickled Red Onions, for
serving (see page 78
for a recipe; optional)

1 Combine oil, chipotles, garlic, small chopped onion, and juice in a blender and purée until smooth. Transfer to a large bowl, and add steaks, tossing to coat in marinade; season generously with salt and pepper. Cover with plastic wrap and let marinate at room temperature for 1 hour or in the refrigerator for up to 4 hours.

2 Build a medium-hot fire in a charcoal grill or heat a gas grill to medium hot. (Alternatively, heat a grill pan over medium-high heat.) Brush marinade from steaks and transfer to the grill; cook, flipping once, until charred and cooked to desired doneness, about 6 minutes for medium-rare. Transfer steaks to a cutting board and let rest for 5 minutes.

3 Meanwhile, place jalapeño and onion on grill, and cook, turning as needed, until charred and softened, about 10 minutes. Transfer vegetables to a cutting board and finely chop; transfer to a serving bowl. Finely chop steaks and toss with grilled vegetables in bowl. Serve in tortillas, with lime wedges, tomatillo salsa, and pickled onions, if you like, on the side.

Cooking Note *Hanger steak also works well in this dish, as will most any other cut of steak.*

RED CHILE ENCHILADAS

Enchiladas de Mole Rojo

SERVES 6-8

These classic Oaxacan enchiladas are stuffed with chicken and bathed
in a sweet guajillo chile sauce.

3	oz. dried guajillo chiles
6	plum tomatoes, cored
4	cloves garlic, peeled
2	serrano chiles, stemmed
½	large white onion, cut into 1" slices, plus 1 medium white onion, minced
1	cup plus 1 tbsp. canola oil
2	cups chicken stock
1	tsp. dried oregano, preferably Mexican
1	tsp. dried thyme
¼	tsp. freshly ground black pepper
1	slice white bread, toasted and torn into small pieces
¼	cup light brown sugar
2	tbsp. fresh lime juice
	Kosher salt, to taste
18	corn tortillas
1½	cups shredded cooked chicken
¾	cup crumbled Cotija or feta cheese, plus more to garnish
	Sliced white onion rings, to garnish
	Chopped cilantro, to garnish

1 Heat a 12" skillet over high heat, and add chiles. Cook, turning once, until lightly toasted, about 2 minutes. Transfer to a bowl and cover with 3 cups boiling water, let sit until rehydrated, about 20 minutes. Drain chiles, reserving soaking liquid, and remove stems and seeds. Transfer chiles to a blender along with 1½ cups soaking liquid; purée until smooth and set chile purée aside.

2 Return skillet to heat, and add tomatoes, garlic, chiles, and onion slices. Cook, turning as needed, until vegetables are lightly charred all over, about 14 minutes for the tomatoes, chiles, and onion, 8 minutes for the garlic. Transfer vegetables to a bowl and let cool. Return skillet to heat and add 1 tbsp. oil; add chile purée and cook, stirring constantly, until thickened to a paste, about 12 minutes. Return paste to blender along with vegetables, stock, oregano, thyme, pepper, and bread; purée until smooth, at least 2 minutes. Pour through a fine strainer into skillet and return skillet to medium-high heat; bring to a boil, and then reduce heat to medium-low, and cook until slightly reduced, about 6 minutes. Stir in sugar and juice, season with salt, and keep enchilada sauce warm in skillet.

3 Heat remaining oil in a 12" skillet over medium-high heat. Working in batches, grasp tortillas with tongs and fry in oil until pliable, 30 seconds each. Transfer tortillas to skillet with enchilada sauce and toss to coat in sauce, then place on a work surface. Divide chicken, cheese, and minced onion among tortillas and roll each tortilla around chicken to form tight rolls.

4 To serve, transfer enchiladas to a large serving platter, and sprinkle with more cheese, onion rings, and cilantro.

MEXICAN SCRAMBLED EGGS

Huevos a la Mexicana

SERVES 4–6

This quick, satisfying breakfast dish is made a la *Mexicana* with red tomatoes, white onion, and green jalapeño, which mirror the colors of the Mexican flag.

3   tbsp. canola oil

1   small white onion, finely chopped

1   jalapeño, stemmed, seeded, and finely chopped

1   plum tomato, cored, seeded, and finely chopped

    Kosher salt and freshly ground black pepper, to taste

2   tbsp. thinly sliced cilantro leaves

8   eggs, lightly beaten

    Warm corn tortillas, for serving

1 Heat oil in a 12" skillet over medium-high heat. Add onion, jalapeño, and tomato, season with salt and pepper, and cook, stirring, until soft, about 6 minutes.

2 Add cilantro and eggs, and cook, folding eggs over in large curds occasionally, until cooked through, about 4 minutes. Transfer to serving plates and serve with tortillas, if you like.

Cooking Note *The night before you make this dish, chop the vegetables and cilantro, and store them in the refrigerator in separate bowls. All you'll need to do the next morning is crack some eggs and fire up the skillet.*

PORK IN RED CHILE SAUCE

Asado de Bodas

SERVES 8–10

This sumptuous stew, a favorite in the state of Zacatecas, makes a satisfying supper when paired with Mexican rice or warm tortillas.

8	dried New Mexico chiles
2	dried guajillo chiles
½	cup almonds
½	cup unsalted peanuts
2	oz. Mexican chocolate, roughly chopped
½	cup raisins
¼	tsp. ground cumin
¼	tsp. ground cinnamon
⅛	tsp. ground cloves
3	cloves garlic, smashed
¼	small yellow onion, chopped
	Kosher salt and freshly ground black pepper, to taste
1	tbsp. canola oil
2	lb. boneless pork shoulder, cut into 1" chunks
	Lime wedges, for serving (optional)

1 Heat a 12" skillet over high heat and add chiles. Cook, turning, until lightly toasted, about 3 minutes. Transfer to a bowl and cover with 5 cups boiling water; let sit until chiles soften, about 20 minutes. Drain, reserving soaking liquid, and remove stems and seeds. Transfer chiles and reserved soaking liquid to a blender and set aside. Return skillet to heat and add almonds and peanuts; cook, stirring often, until lightly toasted, about 3 minutes. Transfer nuts to blender, and add chocolate, raisins, cumin, cinnamon, cloves, garlic, and onion; season with salt and pepper, and purée until smooth. Set sauce aside.

2 Heat oil in skillet over medium-high heat. Season pork with salt and pepper and, working in batches, add to skillet and cook, turning as needed, until pork is browned on all sides, about 12 minutes.

3 Stir the sauce into the pork and bring to a boil. Reduce the heat to medium-low and cook, stirring occasionally, until pork is tender, about 1 hour. Divide among soup bowls, and serve with lime wedges, if you like.

Cooking Note *This dish's mole-like sauce can be prepared days in advance and stirred into the pot with the browned pork to cook before serving.*

PORK RIBS IN SPICY TOMATILLO SAUCE

Costillas de Puerco en Salsa Verde

SERVES 6-8

A tart, fruity sauce offsets the richness of bone-in pork ribs
in this luscious dish.

4   oz. tomatillos,
    husked and rinsed

2   jalapeños, stemmed

2   cups lightly-packed
    cilantro leaves

1   tsp. sugar

4   cloves garlic

2   lb. pork baby back ribs,
    separated into individual
    ribs

1   tsp. dried oregano,
    preferably Mexican

6   cloves garlic, roughly
    chopped

1   large yellow onion, cut
    lengthwise into 8 wedges

1   medium zucchini, cut
    into 2" x ½" batons

    Kosher salt and freshly
    ground black pepper,
    to taste

    Warm tortillas,
    for serving

    Tomato and Chile Salsa,
    for serving (see page 31
    for a recipe; optional)

1 Place tomatillos and jalapeños in a 4-qt. saucepan and cover with water by 1". Bring to a boil over high heat; cook until slightly soft, about 5 minutes. Drain vegetables, and set aside to cool to room temperature. Place in a food processor along with cilantro, sugar, and garlic, and pulse until finely chopped but not puréed; set sauce aside.

2 Bring pork and 4 cups water to a boil in a 6-qt. saucepan over medium-high heat. Cook, stirring occasionally, until all water evaporates, about 1 hour and 15 minutes. Continue cooking pork, stirring often, until it begins to caramelize on the outside, about 10 minutes. Add oregano, garlic, and onion, and cook, stirring, until soft and lightly browned, about 10 minutes. Add sauce and 4 cups water, bring to a boil, and then reduce heat to medium-low; cook, stirring occasionally, until pork is tender and sauce is thickened, about 30 minutes. Add zucchini, and cook until warmed through, about 5 minutes. Season with salt and pepper.

3 Divide pork and sauce among serving bowls and garnish with a drizzling of salsa, if you like. Serve with tortillas.

Cooking Note *Pork shoulder, cut into 1" cubes, or even pork necks, can also be used in this hearty stew in place of the ribs.*

CREAMY CHICKEN AND CHILE ENCHILADAS

Enchiladas Suizas

SERVES 4–6

This dish, smothered in melted cheese, originated at Sanborns coffee shop in Mexico City in 1950. Its name, "Swiss enchiladas," alludes to its dairy-rich nature.

1½ lb. tomatillos, husks removed, rinsed

2 serrano chiles, stemmed

1 cup roughly chopped cilantro

1 cup sour cream

½ tsp. cumin seeds, toasted

4 cloves garlic, roughly chopped

2 poblano chiles, roasted, peeled, seeded, and roughly chopped

Kosher salt and freshly ground black pepper, to taste

3 cups cooked shredded chicken

8 corn tortillas

1½ cups shredded Chihuahua or mozzarella cheese

1 Arrange an oven rack 4" from the broiler and heat broiler to high. Place tomatillos and serranos on a foil-lined baking sheet and broil, turning as needed, until blackened all over, about 10 minutes. Let cool for about 10 minutes, and then peel and discard skins. Transfer to a blender along with cilantro, sour cream, cumin, garlic, poblanos, and 1 cup boiling water; season with salt and pepper, and purée until smooth. Set sauce aside.

2 Place chicken in a bowl and toss with 1 cup sauce until evenly coated. Divide sauced chicken evenly among tortillas and roll tortillas around chicken to create tight rolls. Pour about 1 cup sauce in the bottom of a 9" x 13" baking dish and place tortilla rolls in dish, seam side down, creating one row down the center of the dish. Pour remaining sauce over rolls, and cover evenly with cheese.

3 Heat oven to 375°. Bake enchiladas until sauce is bubbling and cheese is melted on top, about 25 minutes. Remove from oven and let cool for 10 minutes. Serve immediately with plenty of sauce from the dish.

Cooking Note *The sauce can be prepared up to three days in advance and refrigerated. All you have to do for dinner, then, is roll the tortillas around the chicken and place them in the baking dish with the sauce and cheese.*

CRISPY POTATO TACOS

Tacos de Papa

SERVES 8

Great for a meatless meal, these filling tacos are stuffed with
cumin-spiced potatoes and fried until crunchy.

1	tbsp. finely chopped cilantro
½	tsp. dried oregano, preferably Mexican
½	tsp. sugar
2	ripe tomatoes, cored
2	red jalapeños, stemmed
1	clove garlic, smashed, plus 2 cloves, minced
1	lb. russet potatoes, peeled
1	tbsp. unsalted butter
2	tsp. kosher salt
1	tsp. freshly ground black pepper, plus more to taste
1	tsp. ground cumin
½	cup canola oil
18	corn tortillas
	Thinly sliced green cabbage and tomatoes, and crumbled Cotija or feta cheese, for serving

1 Purée cilantro, oregano, sugar, tomatoes, jalapeños, smashed garlic, and ⅔ cup water in a blender until smooth; set sauce aside. Bring a 4-qt. saucepan of salted water to a boil, add potatoes, and cook until tender, about 25 minutes. Drain potatoes and transfer to a large bowl. Add minced garlic, butter, salt, pepper, and cumin, and mash until smooth. Set potato mixture aside.

2 Heat oil in a 12" skillet over medium-high heat. Spread 1 heaping tbsp. of potato mixture over half of each tortilla, and fold over to form a taco. Working in batches, add tacos to oil and fry, turning once, until golden brown and crisp, about 3 minutes. (Use tongs to hold each taco closed while it fries, so that it stays folded and does not spill its filling.)

3 Stuff cabbage, tomatoes, and Cotija into tacos and serve with the sauce on the side.

Cooking Note *For a quicker version of this recipe, fry the flat tortillas until crisp, then top them with the potato filling and condiments to make tostadas.*

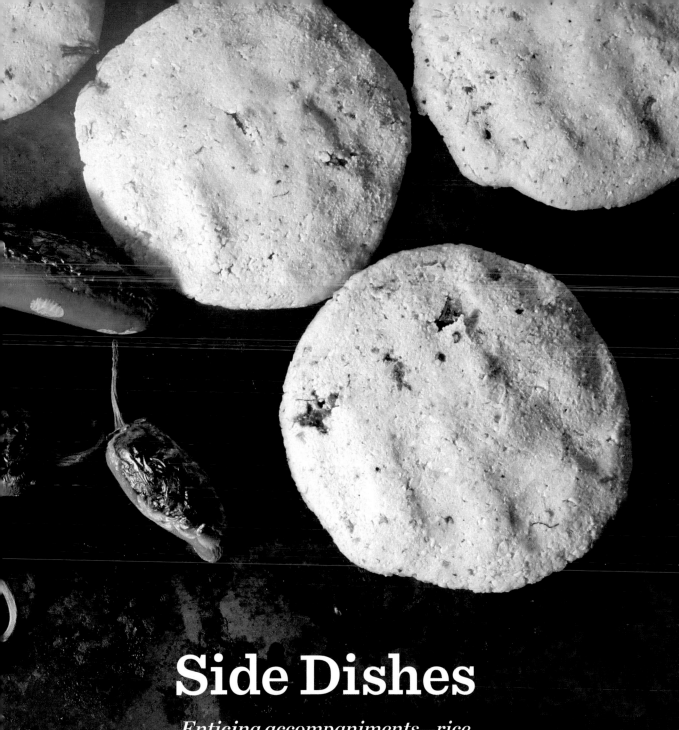

Side Dishes

*Enticing accompaniments—rice
and beans, roasted chiles, and other
vegetables—round out a Mexican meal;
each takes just a few steps to prepare.*

SAUTÉED POTATOES AND CHILES

Papas con Rajas

SERVES 4

This savory, substantial dish makes a terrific accompaniment
to most any type of roasted meat.

12	oz. small Yukon gold potatoes, cut into ¼"-thick discs
3	poblano chiles
3	tbsp. canola oil
1	medium white onion, thinly sliced
3	cloves garlic, finely chopped
4	sprigs cilantro, roughly chopped
	Kosher salt and freshly ground black pepper, to taste

1 Place potatoes in a 4-qt. saucepan and cover with water by 1"; bring to a boil over high heat, and cook until just tender, about 20 minutes. Drain, and set aside. Meanwhile, heat broiler to high. Place poblano chiles on a foil-lined baking sheet and broil, turning as needed, until blackened all over, about 20 minutes. Transfer chiles to a bowl, and let cool. Peel and discard chile skins, stems, and seeds, and thinly slice lengthwise; set aside.

2 Heat oil in a 12" skillet over medium-high heat. Add onion, and cook, stirring, until slightly caramelized, about 12 minutes. Add garlic and chiles, and cook, stirring, until heated through, about 2 minutes. Add potatoes, and cook, stirring, until potatoes are very tender, about 10 minutes.

3 Remove from heat and stir in cilantro; season with salt and pepper, and serve warm.

Cooking Note *If you have a gas stove, you can roast the chiles directly over the flame until charred. Simply grasp them with tongs and progressively turn them as they blacken.*

PICKLED RED ONIONS

Escabeche de Cebolla

MAKES ABOUT 1¾ CUPS

Red onions soak up the flavors of oregano and cumin in this
relish, a beloved condiment of the Yucatán peninsula.

1 tbsp. kosher salt

1 large red onion, thinly
   sliced lengthwise

1 tsp. whole black
   peppercorns

1 tsp. dried oregano

1 tsp. cumin seeds

3 cloves garlic, peeled
   and halved lengthwise

1 fresh bay leaf

1½ cups red wine vinegar

1 In a bowl, toss salt and onion together; let sit until onion
releases some of its liquid, about 15 minutes.

2 Transfer onions with salt and liquid to a glass jar along
with peppercorns, oregano, cumin, garlic, and bay leaf
and pour over vinegar; seal with a lid. Refrigerate at least
4 hours before using.

Cooking Note *Yellow or white onions or shallots will work
just as well for this relish, although they won't have the same
appealing pink color.*

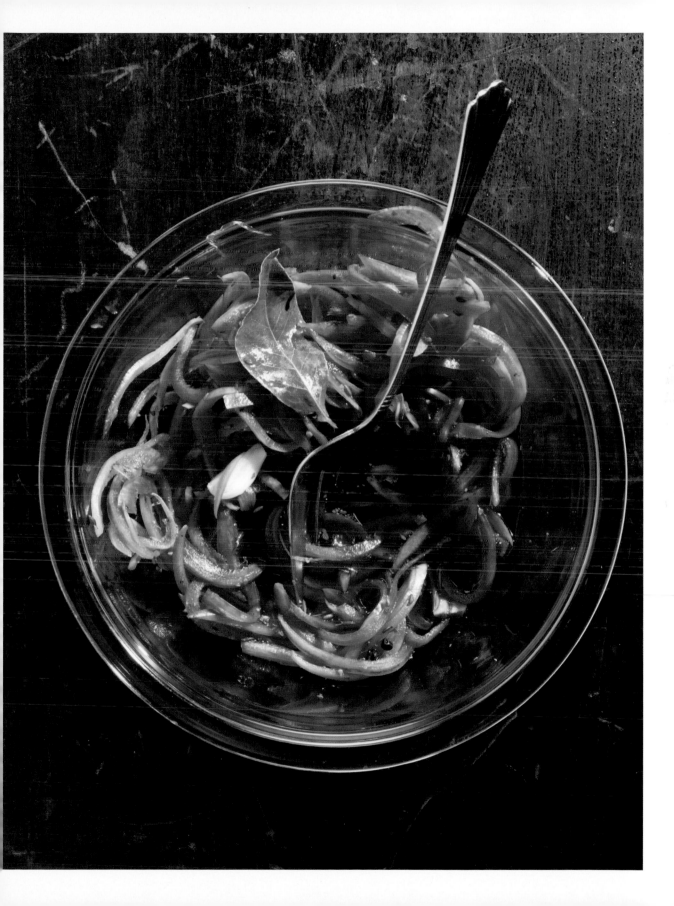

MEXICAN RICE

Arroz a la Mexicana

SERVES 6–8

This vibrant side dish gets its complex flavor from chicken
stock and its hint of heat from serrano chiles.

1	cup chicken stock
1	15-oz. can whole peeled tomatoes in juice
2	tbsp. canola oil
2	serrano chiles, halved lengthwise, seeds removed
2	cloves garlic, minced
½	small yellow onion, minced
2	cups long-grain white rice
1	cup frozen, thawed peas
	Kosher salt and freshly ground black pepper, to taste

1 Place stock and tomatoes with juice in a blender and purée until smooth; set tomato mixture aside.

2 Heat oil in a 4-qt. saucepan over medium high heat. Add chiles, garlic, and onion, and cook, stirring, until soft, about 4 minutes. Add rice and cook, stirring occasionally, until golden brown, about 6 minutes. Stir in tomato mixture and peas, season with salt and pepper, and reduce heat to low. Cook, covered, until rice is tender and has absorbed all the liquid, about 15 minutes. Remove rice from heat, and gently fluff with a fork before serving.

Cooking Note *Canned tomatoes give this rice a richer red color; but if you have fresh, ripe tomatoes on hand in the summer, by all means, use them instead.*

STEWED BEANS WITH PICO DE GALLO

Frijoles de la Olla

SERVES 6-8

This simple side dish can be made with nearly any type of legume: Black beans, navy beans, and even chickpeas are fine substitutes for the pinto beans.

2 cups dried pinto beans

1 clove garlic, smashed

1 whole jalapeño, plus ½ stemmed, seeded, minced

½ whole small white onion, plus ¼ small onion, minced

Kosher salt and freshly ground black pepper, to taste

¼ cup chopped cilantro

1 tomato, cored, seeded, and finely chopped

1 Bring beans, garlic, whole jalapeño, ½ whole onion, and 8 cups water to a boil in a 4-qt. saucepan over high heat. Reduce heat to medium-low, season with salt and pepper, and cook, covered and stirring occasionally, until beans are just tender, about 1 hour 45 minutes.

2 Meanwhile, make a pico de gallo by stirring remaining minced jalapeño, minced onion, cilantro, and tomato in a small bowl until combined.

3 Ladle beans into serving bowls and top with pico de gallo.

Cooking Note *If you end up with leftovers of this dish, simply mash them and fry them in a skillet with a quarter cup of oil for quick refried beans the next day.*

BLISTERED SERRANO CHILES WITH CARAMELIZED ONIONS

Chiles Toreados

SERVES 4

These pan-roasted chiles and onions make a great relish for tacos.

12	serrano chiles, halved lengthwise
2	tbsp. canola oil
1	medium white onion, thinly sliced lengthwise
	Kosher salt, to taste
¼	cup chicken stock or water
	Juice of 1 lime

1 Heat a 12" skillet over high heat. Add chiles, and cook, stirring occasionally, until charred all over, about 14 minutes. Add oil and onion, season with salt, and cook, stirring occasionally, until onion is soft and slightly charred, about 8 minutes.

2 Add stock or water and juice to skillet, and stir, scraping bottom, until liquid is half evaporated, about 2 minutes. Remove from the heat and serve warm.

Cooking Note *For a less spicy dish, remove the seeds and ribs from the chiles before cooking them.*

Desserts & Drinks

*Rich, contrasting ingredients—tropical fruits,
unrefined brown sugar, cinnamon, and other spices—
make these easy desserts and drinks irresistible.*

CHURROS

MAKES 34 FRITTERS

Pueblan native Ruben Ortega, the executive pastry chef at Backstreet
Cafe in Houston, Texas, shared his recipe for these long, fluted fritters.
In Mexico, they are often served with thick, hot chocolate for dunking.

6   tbsp. unsalted butter

1   tsp. kosher salt

1   tsp. vanilla extract

1   stick cinnamon,
     preferably Mexican
     canela

2¼   cups flour

1   egg

2   cups sugar

1   tbsp. ground cinnamon,
     preferably Mexican
     canela

     Canola oil, for frying

1 Bring butter, salt, vanilla, cinnamon, and 2¼ cups
water to a boil in a 4-qt. saucepan over medium-high heat.
Remove and discard cinnamon, and then add flour; cook,
stirring constantly with a wooden spoon, until a smooth
dough forms, about 5 minutes. Transfer dough to a bowl
and add egg; stir vigorously until dough is smooth. Transfer
dough to a piping bag fitted with ⅜" star tip and set aside.
Meanwhile, combine sugar and cinnamon in a large brown
paper bag or a 9" x 13" baking dish; set aside.

2 Pour oil to a depth of 2" in an 8-qt. Dutch oven and heat
over medium-high heat until a deep-fry thermometer reads
400°. Working in batches, hold piping bag above oil, and
pipe about four 6" lengths of dough, severing each from the
piping bag with scissors. Fry fritters until golden brown,
about 2 minutes.

3 Transfer to paper towels to drain briefly, and then transfer
to bag or dish with cinnamon-sugar and quickly shake or roll
in sugar until evenly coated. Repeat with remaining dough in
piping bag. Serve churros immediately.

Cooking Note *Tossing the fritters with the cinnamon-
sugar in a large brown paper sack makes for easier coating
and cleanup.*

SWEET POTATOES STEWED IN SYRUP

Camotes

SERVES 6

This sweet and citrusy dish, bathed in a syrup made with *piloncillo,* or unrefined brown sugar, can be served as a side dish or as a dessert.

1   lb. piloncillo sugar, roughly chopped, or 3 cups packed brown sugar

1   cup fresh orange juice

2   lb. sweet potatoes, peeled and cut into 1½" chunks

1   3" stick cinnamon, preferably Mexican canela

1   1" piece ginger, peeled and finely chopped

    Peel of 1 orange, white pith removed, roughly chopped

2   tsp. fresh lime juice

    Kosher salt, to taste

1 Heat the piloncillo, orange juice, and ½ cup water in a 6-qt. saucepan over medium-high heat, stirring often, until dissolved, 10 minutes. Add the sweet potatoes, cinnamon, ginger, and orange peel; reduce heat to medium-low, and cook, covered and stirring occasionally, until potatoes are tender, about 30 minutes.

2 Using a slotted spoon, transfer sweet potatoes to a large serving dish, and continue cooking liquid until reduced to a syrupy consistency, about 30 minutes more.

3 Stir in lime juice and a pinch of salt, and pour syrup over sweet potatoes. Serve warm or at room temperature.

Cooking Note *Butternut or acorn squash, pumpkin, and even carrots can substitute or supplement the sweet potatoes in this recipe.*

CACTUS FRUITS

In late summer in Mexico, prickly pear cactus fruits, or *tunas*, are everywhere—eaten as snacks and appearing in candies, drinks, and jams. *Tunas* can be used as you would an apple—in salads, for example, or in tarts. The nubs on the skin contain spines, but these are easily removed by slicing off the ends of the fruit, making lengthwise incisions, and peeling back the rind to reveal the luscious flesh. Here are a few varieties you might find in Mexican markets in the States: ❶ The widely available **cardona** has soft seeds and a bittersweet flavor. ❷ The floral **cuerno de venado**'s high water content and small seed size make it a favorite for snacking. ❸ The **platanera** has a bananalike flavor. ❹ The **cristalina,** also known as *zarca*, is juicy, crisp, and tastes like a peach. ❺ The **naranjona** has a honey-sweet, subtly spicy flavor. ❻ The wild **xoconostle** has a sour, edible peel that is sometimes used in savory stews. ❼ The **Juana** (sometimes called *roja*) contains large, chewy seeds and tart, crimson flesh. ❽ The **roja pelona,** which is kiwilike in flavor, is free of thorns.

MEXICAN BREAD PUDDING
WITH RUM SAUCE
SERVES 8–10

This Mexican take on a Cajun-style bread pudding is studded with cubes of squash and plump raisins. The recipe comes from chef Susana Trilling of Seasons of My Heart Cooking School in Oaxaca.

FOR THE BREAD PUDDING:

- 10 tbsp. unsalted butter, melted, plus more
- ¾ cup raisins
- 4 cups milk
- 1½ cups sugar
- 2 tbsp. Grand Marnier
- 2 tsp. vanilla extract
- 1 tsp. ground cinnamon,
- 1 tsp. ground nutmeg
- ¼ tsp. kosher salt
- 4 eggs, lightly beaten
- 1 medium butternut squash, peeled and cut into ½" cubes
- 6 oz. stale white country bread, cut into 1" cubes

FOR THE SAUCE:

- 1½ cups packed dark brown sugar
- 8 tbsp. unsalted butter
- ½ cup heavy cream
- ¼ cup rum
- ¼ tsp. kosher salt
- Whipped cream, to serve

1 Make the bread pudding: Heat the oven to 350°. Grease a 9" x 13" glass or ceramic baking dish with a little butter and set aside. Place the raisins in a small bowl and cover with boiling water; let sit for 10 minutes.

2 Meanwhile, whisk together the melted butter, milk, sugar, Grand Marnier, vanilla, cinnamon, nutmeg, salt, and eggs in a large bowl until smooth. Drain the raisins and stir into the custard mixture along with the squash and bread; let sit for 10 minutes. Pour mixture into prepared baking dish and cover with aluminum foil. Bake for 50 minutes, uncover, and continue baking until bread pudding is golden brown, about 1 hour more.

3 Make the sauce: Bring the sugar, butter, heavy cream, rum, and salt to a boil in a 2-qt. saucepan over medium-high heat, and cook until the sugar dissolves and sauce thickens slightly, about 5 minutes; set aside and keep warm.

4 To serve, spoon bread pudding into serving bowls, drizzle with sauce, and top with a dollop of whipped cream.

Cooking Note *Acorn squash, pumpkin, and even sweet potatoes can be substituted for the butternut squash here.*

MANGO-CHILE ICE POPS

Paletas de Mango con Chile

MAKES 8 ICE POPS

Paletas, or ice pops, are a beloved frozen treat in Mexico; mango-chile is just one of hundreds of flavors made at paleterias across the country.

1	cup store-bought mango juice or nectar
¼	cup sugar
2	tsp. fresh lemon juice
1	tsp. ancho chile powder
1	large mango, peeled, seeded, and cut into small cubes

1 Heat mango juice, sugar, lemon juice, and ½ cup water in a 1-qt. saucepan over medium-high heat, and stir until sugar dissolves. Transfer mixture to a bowl and refrigerate until chilled.

2 Stir chile powder and cubed mango into the chilled mixture and pour into eight 3-oz. ice-pop molds. Insert a Popsicle stick into each mold and freeze until pops are solid, about 3 hours more.

3 To release ice pops from molds, run the bottoms of the molds briefly under cold water.

Cooking Note *If mango isn't available, substitute papaya, passion fruit, or even blackberries and their juices in these ice pops.*

MICHELADA

MAKES 1 DRINK

The name of this refreshing cocktail combines the Mexican slang for "cold beer," *chelada,* and the moniker of the bartender, Michel Esper, who is said to have created it at the Club Deportivo Portofino in San Luis Potosí, Mexico.

1	lime wedge
	Kosher salt
1	tbsp. lime juice
¼	tsp. worcestershire
¼	tsp. Mexican hot sauce, such as Cholula
1	bottle Mexican lager, such as Tecate
1	pickled jalapeño

1 Rub the rim of a tall glass with the lime wedge. Dip the rim of the glass into a small bowl of kosher salt. Add lime juice, worcestershire, and hot sauce to the glass, and then add cracked ice to half-fill the glass.

2 Pour in beer just shy of the salt rim, and stir to combine. Garnish with a pickled jalapeño, if you like.

Cooking Note *To make Micheladas for a party, multiply and mix all the ingredients, except for the ice and beer, in a pitcher. As guests arrive, pour shots of the mix into glasses, and fill with ice and beer.*

CLASSIC SHAKEN MARGARITA

MAKES 2 DRINKS

Tequila, a spirit made from Mexico's blue agave plant, has a brisk, briny flavor that pairs well with tart lime in this simple but delicious classic.

4 oz. silver tequila, such as Herradura

1½ oz. fresh lime juice

1 oz. Cointreau

½ oz. simple syrup

1 Combine tequila, lime juice, Cointreau, simple syrup and ½ cup crushed ice in a cocktail shaker; cover and shake until chilled, about 15 seconds.

2 Strain into 2 small chilled tumblers or cocktail glasses and fill with ice.

Cooking Note *Avoid using sour mix to make a margarita. High-quality tequila and fresh lime juice are key to this simple cocktail's complex flavor.*

A server at a restaurant called Los Angeles in Puebla, Mexico.

THE MEXICAN PANTRY

Cilantro

This pungent herb isn't native to Mexico—it arrived from the Mediterranean with the Spanish in the 16th century—but it's become an indispensible ingredient in regional cuisines throughout the country. Mexican cooks use the flavorful upper stems as well as the leaves, chopping them coarsely and adding them to cooked sauces, soups, and stews, as well as raw salsas. Chopped cilantro is also scattered raw over an infinite number of savory dishes, to which it adds bright color and a distinctive flavor.

Corn Tortillas

Soft corn tortillas are rolled and sauced to make enchiladas, broken up and fried for tortilla chips, and set out, tableside, for making ad-hoc tacos out of everything from grilled steak to scrambled eggs. It's easy to make your own (see page 56 for a recipe), but supermarkets also carry them. Look for local brands (often sold unrefrigerated), as they will be freshest. Before serving, heat them in a dry, cast-iron skillet over medium-high heat, cooking one tortilla at a time, turning once, until lightly blistered and charred in spots, about 1½ minutes per side. Wrap in a clean kitchen towel to keep warm.

Pinto Beans

Native to northern Mexico, these small, earthy beans, which are mottled beige when raw, turn reddish-brown with cooking. Hearty, nutritious, and flavorful, they're the basis of refried beans as well as long-simmered soups. If you don't have time to soak and cook dried beans, canned versions, which are just as easily found at the supermarket, make a good, quick substitute.

THE MEXICAN PANTRY

Continued

Fideo

The thin, long Mexican noodles called *fideo* are the basis for beloved comfort foods like the noodle casserole known as *sopa seca* (literally "dry soup"; see page 55 for a recipe). Pasta came to Mexico in the late 19th century, when European cuisine was in vogue. The dried wheat noodles, sold in bundles, are typically broken up and fried in oil in a hot pan before being incorporated into a dish. Angel hair pasta, vermicelli, or spaghetti can be used instead.

Key Lime

Ping-Pong ball–size Key limes, or Mexican limes, which turn yellow when ripe, are prized for their dynamic acidity—at its greatest when the fruit is green and unripe—and copious juice. They will keep, loosely wrapped in a plastic bag in the refrigerator crisper, for 10 to 14 days. They're available at most grocery stores, but if you can't find them, Persian limes—the most common supermarket variety—are a fine substitute.

Mexican Chocolate

Coarser than most American baking chocolates, Mexican chocolate typically contains cinnamon, ground almonds, and granulated sugar. It is sold in tablet form and is not meant for eating out of hand. Instead, it is melted and combined with milk or cream to make drinking chocolate, stirred into moles, and used to enrich all manner of other preparations, both sweet and savory. It's widely available at most supermarkets and Mexican grocery stores.

Squash Blossoms

Thanks to consistently warm climates in many parts of the country, squash blossoms are available year-round in Mexico, where they are stuffed with cheese and fried, cooked inside quesadillas, stirred into soups, laid atop salads, and used as a filling for tacos. You can find them in farmers' markets and some specialty grocery stores in the spring and summer, though you can also grow your own.

Cotija Cheese

This hard, aged cows' milk cheese has a sharp, feta-like flavor. It's often crumbled and sprinkled over beans and rice, soups, tacos, and other dishes, where it adds texture and a salty tang. Though most Mexican groceries carry the cheese (it's sometimes labeled *queso añejo* or *queso seca),* as do well-stocked supermarkets, you can also substitute feta or ricotta salata.

Avocado

Rich avocados are ubiquitous in Mexico. The star ingredient in guacamole is also sliced into salads and on sandwiches, used as a garnish, and incorporated into sauces. The medium-size Haas variety, prized for its dense, buttery flesh, is ideal for guacamole. It has pebbled skin that turns practically black when fully ripe. When shopping, select avocados that yield when gently pressed; avoid ones that have soft spots or whose skin has started to separate from the flesh. (You can also buy unripe avocados and ripen them in a paper bag at room temperature.)

THE MEXICAN PANTRY

Continued

Jalapeño

Hundreds of varieties of fresh chile pepper are used in Mexican cooking; spicy jalapeños *(Capsicum annuum)* are among the most popular. The chiles are used to perk up salsas and other foods, and pickled and enjoyed as a condiment. The piquancy of all chiles is concentrated in the white membrane that holds the seeds to its flesh; to tame the heat, remove the seeds and ribs before using.

Canela

Canela, as true cinnamon is called in Spanish, is made from the oil-rich bark of a Sri Lankan tree of the species *Cinnamomum verum.* It's softer, flakier, and subtler than the hard, rolled quills of cassia often sold as "cinnamon" in most American grocery stores, making it ideal as a flavoring in complex moles and delicate desserts. It's widely available in Mexican grocery stores. Once ground, it loses flavor quickly, so grind it in a spice mill as needed.

Tomatillo

These light green, walnut-size relatives of the tomato impart a sweet-tart, citrusy flavor to salsas and sauces. Each tomatillo is encased in a papery, lantern-shaped husk that must be discarded before cooking the fruit or puréeing it for raw salsa. Tomatillos are available in most supermarkets. Look for ones that fill their husks, and whose fruit is firm and unbruised; they will keep in the refrigerator for several weeks.

Crema

A mild-tasting cultured cream with a slightly viscous consistency, *crema* is used to enrich soups and sauces and to garnish enchiladas, soups, noodle casseroles, and any number of other dishes. Most Latin American markets and some grocery stores carry jarred *crema*, but you can also substitute crème fraîche or sour cream; thin the latter with a little milk or heavy cream, so it has a better consistency for drizzling.

Chorizo

Unlike the cured, oftentimes firm Spanish sausage of the same name, Mexican-style chorizo is a fresh pork sausage. Laced with dried chile peppers, vinegar, paprika, cilantro, and garlic, and then cooked, the mildly spicy sausage is crumbled atop everything from fried potatoes to tacos. It's widely available, both in a casing and loose, in Mexican grocery stores.

Cumin Seeds

Throughout Mexico, whole cumin seeds are ground and added along with other spices to marinades, moles, and stews. Though Mexican cooks usually pan-toast the seeds before grinding them to enhance their flavor, cumin tends to be used sparingly so that it does not overpower a dish. Whole seeds, which can be ground in a spice grinder, are readily available in supermarkets. But it's even simpler to use pre-ground cumin. Ground cumin loses its flavor over time, though, so use it within six months of purchasing.

MEZCAL

Mezcal, the national spirit of Mexico, has been made since pre-Columbian times by roasting, crushing, and fermenting the heart of the spiny agave plant (also known as maguey), then distilling the resulting mash. Among the many distinct regional styles, the one made near the town of Tequila, in the state of Jalisco, is the most popular. Tequila, which may be made with only the blue agave, a type of maguey, is increasingly made through mechanized processes. While the spirit is smoother than traditional mezcal, it's also less expressive of the place where it's made and the plant itself. Aficionados seek out handcrafted spirits, made by methods that haven't changed in generations. On the bracing end of these are the young, clear joven mezcals. Great in cocktails, in Mexico they're often enjoyed neat, accompanied by orange slices and chile-laced *sal de gusano* (worm salt). Among these is the crisp, clean **Del Maguey Chichicapa** with its herbal flavors and sharp minerality. **Sombra,** a mild joven, kicks off with scents of ash, wet earth, and grass, but tastes of black pepper and sweet citrus. **Del Maguey Tobalá,** made from the prized wild tobalá agave, offers unexpected but harmonious flavors: cake icing and old leather, lime rind and cocoa, beeswax and salted caramel. Mellower, barrel-aged reposados are great for sipping at the end of a meal, like a cognac. **Los Amantes Reposado** calls to mind the high sierra: smoldering pine needles and warm stone. Cereal notes belie **Los Danzantes Reposado's** agave origin; dried corn, puffed rice, and new leather dominate the nose. Its syrupy body brings tastes of maple, pecan, and brown butter. All of these mezcals are readily available now in liquor stores and higher end restaurants in the States.

MEXICAN WINES

Mexico's wine industry is the oldest in the Americas. In 1524, two years after conquering the Aztecs, the Spanish conquistador Hernán Cortés ordered colonists to plant grape vines. Ships sailing from Spain brought cuttings to the New World, where they thrived. Today, 90 percent of Mexican wines are produced on the Baja peninsula, on the country's northwest coast. Baja's Valle de Guadalupe lies 15 miles inland of the city Ensenada, where cooling Pacific breezes and the sheltering Sierra Nevada mountains temper the dry Sonoran heat, resulting in a microclimate that's ideal for growing grapes. Typically, Baja wines have a more rustic nature than bottles produced farther north in California. The water table on the peninsula is slightly saline. You can taste it in reds like the **Paralelo Ensamble Arenal BA II 2008,** a spicy, salty, earthy cabernet-merlot blend that is perfect with *carne asada* and other grilled meats. Also touched by brine but with richer cherry and bacon notes, the cabernet-merlot blend **Viñas Pijoan Leonora 2008** goes great with smoky-sweet mole poblano. **La Trinidad Fauno 2009,** a woody nebbiolo-cabernet-zinfandel blend with hints of tobacco and dark, stewed fruit, stands up to spicy dishes like the pork in red chile sauce, while the funky, peppery, herbaceous **Balché Zinfandel 2008** is a nuanced wine that goes well with everything from chiles rellenos to chicken guisado. Though many Baja reds are blends, the whites are great as single varietals. These run the gamut from the bright, citrus-and-apple **Paralelo Emblema 2010**—a sauvignon blanc to pair with shrimp ceviche—to buttery yet balanced **Monte Xanic Chardonnay,** whose toasted almonds and tropical fruit flavors make it a match for creamy enchiladas suizas.

TABLE OF EQUIVALENTS

The exact equivalents in the following tables have been rounded for convenience.

Liquid and Dry Measurements

U.S.	METRIC
¼ teaspoon	1.25 milliliters
½ teaspoon	2.5 milliliters
1 teaspoon	5 milliliters
1 tablespoon (3 teaspoons)	15 milliliters
1 fluid ounce	30 milliliters
¼ cup	65 milliliters
⅓ cup	80 milliliters
1 cup	235 milliliters
1 pint (2 cups)	480 milliliters
1 quart (4 cups, 32 fluid ounces)	950 milliliters
1 gallon (4 quarts)	3.8 liters
1 ounce (by weight)	28 grams
1 pound	454 grams
2.2 pounds	1 kilogram

Length Measures

U.S.	METRIC
⅛ inch	3 millimeters
¼ inch	6 millimeters
½ inch	12 millimeters
1 inch	2.5 centimeters

Oven Temperatures

FAHRENHEIT	CELSIUS	GAS
250°	120°	½
275°	140°	1
300°	150°	2
325°	160°	3
350°	180°	4
375°	190°	5
400°	200°	6
425°	220°	7
450°	230°	8
475°	240°	9
500°	260°	10

INDEX

ACKNOWLEDGMENTS

We hope the recipes in this book are easy for anyone to make, but we've learned that making a book like this is never easy! I'd like to thank all the people who contributed to *Easy Mexican,* especially the SAVEUR test kitchen staff—Ben Mims and Kellie Evans, and their assistants Jeanna DeMarco, Katharine Hamlin, and Kristin Piegza—for their endless pursuit of recipe perfection. Also Todd Coleman, who not only oversaw the test kitchen but also took the majority of the photographs in this edition. Betsy Andrews put in countless hours making sure the text was poetic, and had excellent support from Gabriella Gershenson and Beth Kracklauer, one of our experts in Mexican food culture. Karen Shimizu wrote the Mexican pantry, in addition to checking all the facts that appear in the book. Dave Weaver designed the pages, and Eric Powell broke away from his day job as *Garden Design* art director to make them pop. Crackerjack photo director Chelsea Lobser sorted through and tracked thousands of photos. And Greg Ferro managed to keep the train on time and on the tracks. I'd also like to thank Terry Newell and Hannah Rahill, as well as their colleagues Amy Marr, Emma Boys, Lauren Charles, and Jennifer Newens who always help us understand the many mysteries of book production. —*James Oseland, Editor-in-Chief*

PHOTOGRAPHY CREDITS

Penny De Los Santos 76; **Landon Nordeman** 90, 94; **James Oseland** 65;
Brenda Weaver (illustrations) 42, 43; all others, **Todd Coleman.**

ISBN 13: 978-1-61628-497-8
ISBN 10: 1-61628-497-8

Design by Dave Weaver

Conceived and produced with SAVEUR by Weldon Owen Inc.
415 Jackson Street, Suite 200, San Francisco, CA 94111
Telephone: 415 291 0100 Fax: 415 291 8841

SAVEUR and Weldon Owen are divisions of **BONNIER**